Writing Journal

Memories, Dreams, and Hopes

A blank journal with
inspiring thoughts on the art of writing by
Susan Polis Schutz
and others

Copyright © 1999 by Stephen Schutz and Susan Polis Schutz. Copyright © 1999 by SPS Studios, Inc. All rights reserved. No part of this book may be reproduced in any manner whatsoever without written permission from the publisher. Manufactured in Korea.

Thanks to the following publishers for permission to reprint excerpts from their publications: Viking Penguin, a division of Penguin Putnam, Inc., for "Work freely and madly..." from THE WRITINGS OF A SAVAGE by Paul Gauguin, translated by Eleanor Levieux. Copyright © 1974 by Editions Gallimard. English translation copyright © 1978 by Viking Penguin. All rights reserved. Used by permission. Pantheon Books, a division of Random House, Inc., for "If you are writing the clearest..." from BIRD BY BIRD: SOME INSTRUCTIONS ON WRITING AND LIFE by Anne Lamott. Copyright © 1994 by Anne Lamott. HarperCollins Publishers for "The writer's duty is..." by William Faulkner from THE HARPER BOOK OF AMERICAN QUOTATIONS by Gorton Carruth and Eugene Ehrlich. Copyright © 1988 by Carruth and Ehrlich Books, Inc. W. W. Norton & Company, Inc. for "The writer enables people to discover..." from HUMAN OPTIONS: AN AUTOBIOGRAPHICAL NOTEBOOK by Norman Cousins. Copyright © 1981 by Norman Cousins. All rights reserved. Reprinted by permission.

Blue Mountain Press®

Why do I write?
I write because
I see something
or touch something
or smell something
or feel something
that I cannot understand
until I try to describe it
in written
words

— Susan Polis Schutz

I feel...

I am taken advantage of by you. In order for just about to get done I either have to do it myself or I have to bug you endlessly.

Things I almost always do:
- Laundry - you don't hang/fold clothes when asked
- Dishes
- Feed dogs
- Clean house (except vaccuum)

Nickelback concert.
- Shalyn
- CJ
- Brandon
- Whitney

New Club: For Girls
- self esteem
- self confidence
- study skills
- homework help
- relationships
- self respect
- post-high sch opportunities
- health issues
- meet one/two times week
- guest speakers
- study sessions

If you dedicate yourself to your writing, and follow the voice of inspiration that constantly whispers to your heart... you will find the gift of words to express the deepest longings and visions in your soul.
— Amelia Johnson

Sing a song
Read a poem
Paint a picture
Dance to the music in your head
Rise up
and touch the stars —
today

— Susan Polis Schutz

Our moments of inspiration are not lost though we have no particular poem to show for them; for those experiences have left an indelible impression, and we are ever and anon reminded of them.

— Henry David Thoreau

To Grow as a Writer...

Find many interests and pursue them
Find out what is important to you
Find out what you are good at
Don't be afraid to make mistakes
Work hard to achieve successes
When things are not going right
don't give up — just try harder

— Susan Polis Schutz

All writers are explorers of new worlds. It takes courage to leave behind what is comfortable and familiar and set out on dangerous voyages of discovery. Their reward is to see new possibilities the rest of us may only dream of.

— Richard St. John

> *Whenever you write, pour all of yourself into it. Draw on everything that has occurred in your life up to this moment and breathe as much of it into your words as possible. Both your life and your writing will start to glow with a powerful inner light.*
>
> — N. R. Halloway

What is life to you?
The butterflies among the tulips
The children rolling down the grassy hills
The sun feeding the seeds of fertility
Finding someone whose sensitive expression
makes you cry...

— Susan Polis Schutz

> One great poet is a
> masterpiece of nature.
> — Percy Bysshe Shelley

People will tell you that you are wrong. It has not and cannot be done! Some will even say you are crazy. But if you feel it is right, pursue your idea, your dream, your creativity. That is what makes new discoveries, beauty, and truth.

— Susan Polis Schutz

Work freely and madly; you will make progress and sooner or later people will learn to recognize your work.... Dream on it and look for the simplest form in which you can express it.

— Paul Gauguin

*What makes people succeed
is the fact that they have confidence in themselves
and a very strong sense of purpose
They never have excuses for not doing something
and always try their hardest for perfection*

— Susan Polis Schutz

If you are writing the clearest, truest words you can find and doing the best you can to understand and communicate, this will shine on paper like its own little lighthouse.

— Anne Lamott

*Good writers can accept and benefit from criticism
and they know when to defend what
    they are doing
They are creative people
who are not afraid to be a little different*
— Susan Polis Schutz

> The writer's duty is... to help man endure by lifting his heart, by reminding him of the courage and honor and hope and pride and compassion and pity and sacrifice which have been the glory of his past.
> — William Faulkner

*If you know what you believe in
and if you stick to these beliefs
life will be easier because you
will have a clear-cut
path to follow*

— Susan Polis Schutz

> To write well is to think well, to feel well, and to render well; it is to possess at once intellect, soul, and taste.
> — Comte de Buffon

*Get close to nature
Your everyday games will be insignificant
Notice the clouds spontaneously forming patterns
and try to do that with your life*

— Susan Polis Schutz

Poetry is the record of the best and happiest moments of the best minds..... A poem is the very image of life expressed in its eternal truth.

— Percy Bysshe Shelley

*Don't compare yourself
to anyone
Be happy to be
the wonderful
unique, very special
person that you are*
— Susan Polis Schutz

There are two worlds: the world that we can measure with line and rule, and the world that we feel with our hearts and imagination.

— Leigh Hunt

Novelists should never allow themselves to weary of the study of real life.
— Charlotte Brontë

Know that there is often hidden in us a dormant poet, always young and alive.

— Alfred de Musset

*Give yourself freedom to try out new things
Don't be so set in your ways that you can't grow*
— Susan Polis Schutz

If I could I would always work in silence and obscurity and let my efforts be known by their results.

— Emily Brontë

Genius is one percent inspiration, ninety-nine percent perspiration.
— Thomas Edison

*If you have a goal in life
that takes a lot of energy
that incurs a great deal of interest
and that is a challenge to you
you will always look
forward to waking up to
see what the new day brings*

— Susan Polis Schutz

I have never thought of writing merely for reputation and honor. What I have in my heart and soul — must find a way out.

— Ludwig van Beethoven

> *People who want to become writers don't talk about writing. They write!*
> — Susan Polis Schutz

The poet's eye, in a fine frenzy rolling,
Doth glance from heaven to earth,
    from earth to heaven;
And as imagination bodies forth
The forms of things unknown, the poet's pen
Turns them to shapes, and gives to airy nothing
A local habitation and a name.

— William Shakespeare

Make each day better than the previous day so that you won't look back to the "old days" as the best. The best day should be today.

— Susan Polis Schutz

> *A word is not a crystal, transparent and unchanged; it is the skin of a living thought and may vary greatly in color and content according to the circumstances and time in which it is used.*
>
> — Oliver Wendell Holmes

*Believe in creativity
as a means of expressing
your true feelings
and as a way of
being spontaneous*
— Susan Polis Schutz

*You must like your work
and always try to get better
You must consider yourself a success
by being proud of doing your best*
— Susan Polis Schutz

*The world of reality has its limits;
the world of imagination is boundless.*

— Jean Jacques Rousseau

Seek out the beautiful things in the world so that you can use these positive forces to create a new and better world.

— Susan Polis Schutz

> *A mind that is stretched by a new experience can never go back to its old dimensions.*
>
> — Oliver Wendell Holmes

I must be true to myself
so I write only when
I am inspired
and I never write
because someone expects me to
— Susan Polis Schutz

> The writer enables people to discover new truths and new possibilities within themselves and to fashion new connections to human experience.
>
> — Norman Cousins

Poetry makes immortal all that is best and most beautiful in the world...
— Percy Bysshe Shelley

*The truth is
a poet writes
everywhere
anywhere or
anytime she is inspired*
— Susan Polis Schutz

Words do more than plant miracle seeds. With you writing them, they can change the world.
— Ashley Rice

**Write your feelings down
Create something based on your feelings
but do not keep them inside**

— Susan Polis Schutz

Do not attempt to adopt the style of any author. Unless you can feel that you can be yourself do not try to be anybody. A poor original is better than a good imitation in literature, if not in other things.

— Ella Wheeler Wilcox

> You must listen to your own voice
> and not be influenced by others
> — Susan Polis Schutz

The torment of every artist's life is to find adequate expression for the vague, terrible unrest that drives him. He is forever searching. He is forever driven on to find an adequate medium to express his thought.

— Elbert Hubbard

Let your spirit lead you
on a path of excitement
and fulfillment
And know that
because you are a
determined and talented person
any dream that you dream
can become a reality

— Susan Polis Schutz